Gordon Wetmore's

Prayers for
Boys and Girls

For Dr. and Mrs Peale
In Friendship
Gordon Wetmore

MATT. 18: 1 - 4   3/17/87

AUTOGRAPHED COPY

Gordon Wetmore's

Prayers for Boys and Girls

Ideals Publishing Corp.
Nashville, Tennessee

Copyright © MCMLXXXVI by Gordon Wetmore
ISBN 0-8249-8156-1

Lord, teach a little child to pray,
And, oh, accept my prayer;
Thou canst hear all the words I say,
For Thou art everywhere.

A little sparrow cannot fall
Unnoticed, Lord, by Thee;
And though I am so young and small,
Thou canst take care of me.

Amen.

Author Unknown

Father, hear my prayer this morning;
Guide my footsteps through this day.
Around my heart with love adorning
Wrap Thy peace so it will stay.

Give me of Thy richest blessing;
Bathe me in Thy golden light.
Let me feel Thy strong hand pressing
Should I need it through the night.

Amen.

Clarice Albritton

Heavenly Father, hear my prayer;
Keep me in Thy loving care.

Guide me through each lovely day
In my work and in my play.

Keep me pure and sweet and true
In everything I say and do.

Amen.

Abbie Burr

Before I rise to meet the day,
I fold my hands and softly say:
Dear Lord, may everything I do
Bring me closer unto You.

Amen.

Rosaleen Schmutz

For flowers that bloom about our feet,
    Father, we thank Thee;
For tender grass so fresh and sweet,
    Father, we thank Thee;
For the songs of bird and hum of bee,
For all things fair we hear or see,
Father in Heaven, we thank Thee.

For this new morning with its light,
    Father, we thank Thee;
For rest and shelter of the night,
    Father, we thank Thee;
For health and food, for love and friends,
For everything Thy goodness sends,
Father in Heaven, we thank Thee.

Amen.

Ralph Waldo Emerson

I thank Thee, Lord, for all Thy
   lovely things,
For singing birds, for trees
   and flowers of spring,
For purple mountains wearing
   crowns of snow
That look across green valleys
   far below.
I thank Thee for Thy presence
   ever near
And constant care that keeps
   us from all fear.

Amen.

Rhea Hendricks

Dear God, be good to me;
The sea is so wide
And my boat is so small.

Amen.

Breton fisherman's prayer

I see the moon,
   and the moon sees me.
God bless the sailors
   on the sea.

Amen.

Author Unknown

Thank You, God, for simple joys
That often come my way;
Those unexpected little things
That brighten up my day.

So many gifts that touch our lives
To cheer us on our way;
Thank You, God, for simple joys
That make the worthwhile day!

Amen.

Kay Hoffman

Teach us, Lord, just how to pray
For guidance in this brand new day.
Fill our hearts with love so true,
With sunshine from the heavens blue.

Hear us, Lord, when we sing
Songs of love and praise to Him.
Surround us, Lord, with Thy grace
That we may someday see Thy face.

Comfort us, Lord, from worldly pain
With gentle tears of falling rain.
Teach us, Lord, just what to say
As we pray for guidance on this day.

Amen.

Judi E. Frost

PALACE

Gordon Wetmore

Teach me to love my neighbor, Lord,
To live as I would have him live.
Teach me the value of friendship,
To give as I would have him give.

Teach me to sing of beauty, Lord,
As found in the heart of a child.
Ever remind me of blessings;
Keep all my thoughts undefiled.

Teach me to serve, that I may be
Humble and fit in Thy sight.
Open my eyes to the dawning;
Guide me through darkness of night.

Amen.

Ellen Rebecca Fenn

God made the sun
And God made the tree;
God made the mountains
And God made me.

I thank You, O God,
For the sun and the tree,
For making the mountains,
And for making me.

Amen.

Leah Gale

Lord, make us glad each day
For all the fun along our way;
For work and games, and sun and showers,
And wind and rain to grow our flowers.

For houses along the busy street,
For family and friends we greet;
For everything we do and see
Is good—because it comes from Thee.

Amen.

Author Unknown

O God, this little prayer
  I pray,
Please take good care
  of things:
Of all the little things
  that walk
Or fly with tiny wings.

For we are in this great
  big world
And sometimes are afraid,
So please take care of all
  the things,
O God, that you have made.

Amen.

George L. Ehrman

Now I wake and see the light;
Thy love was with me through the night.

To Thee I speak again and pray
That Thou wilt lead me all the day.

I ask not for myself alone,
But for Thy children, every one.

Amen.

Author Unknown

The Lord is my shepherd;
I shall not want.
He maketh me to lie down
In green pastures;
He leadeth me
Beside the still waters.
He restoreth my soul;
He leadeth me
In the paths of righteousness,
For His name's sake.
Yea, though I walk through
The valley of the shadow
Of death, I will fear no evil;
For thou art with me.
Thy rod and thy staff
They comfort me.
Thou preparest a table
    before me
In the presence of mine
    enemies;
Thou anointest my head
    with oil;
My cup runneth over.
Surely goodness and mercy
Shall follow me all the days
Of my life; and I will dwell in
The house of the Lord for ever.

Psalm 23

Loving Jesus, meek and
  mild,
Look upon a little child!

Make me gentle as Thou
  art,
Come and live within my
  heart.

Take my childish hand
  in Thine,
Guide these little feet of
  mine.

So shall all my happy days
Sing their pleasant song
  of praise;

And the world shall always
  see
Christ, the holy Child, in
  me.

Amen.

Charles Wesley

Thank You, God, for all Your gifts;
Thank You for Your graces.
Thank You for Your loving care
About us in all places.

Amen.

Rosaleen Schmutz

Dear Lord, watch over us
   today,
And guide our steps along
   the way.
Help us be loving, kind,
   and good,
And do all things we know
   we should.

We pray our thoughts be of
   good cheer,
And hold our family ever
   near.
Help us be loyal, steadfast,
   true,
And "Do to others as
   they'd do."

Amen.

Carol Wedekind

We thank Thee, Father
  up in Heaven,
For all the blessings
  Thou hast given:
For home and friends
  and daily food,
And everything that is
  so good.

We thank Thee for the
  work and play
As we go to school
  each day,
For Jesus' love and
  Jesus' care
That travel with us
  everywhere.

Help us to be both kind
  and true,
To do the thing we
  ought to do.
Keep us free from sin
  and blame,
And save us all in
  Jesus' name.

Amen.

Edwin Osgood Grover

For honeysuckle's fragrance rare,
For new-mown hay that sweetens air;

For katydids that sing at night
And lightning bugs with taillights bright;

For open fires and crackling wood,
For Mom's hot cocoa steaming good;

For sunshine dancing on a rug,
For buttermilk from Grandma's jug;

For meadows green and shady creeks
Where Mr. Frog in gusto speaks;

For old church bells that sweetly ring,
I thank Thee for each little thing!

Amen.

Laurie Wilcox

Dear Lord, as I kneel
  down to pray,
Help me to know Thy
  will today.
Help me to be serene
  and still
And rise to do Thy
  holy will.

Guide all my thoughts
  and deeds today;
Guide every step along
  the way.
And when the day at
  last is through,
Let me be thankful,
  Lord, to You.

Amen.

Elizabeth Ann M. Moore

We thank Thee, Lord,
For birds and flowers,
For trees and winds,
And gentle showers.

We thank Thee
For our clothes and food,
For friends and parents,
Kind and good.

And, Lord, we thank Thee
For our play,
And sleep, when tired
At close of day.

Amen.

Herbert Stoneley

Gordon Wetmore
© 088.

Our Father, who art in Heaven,
Hallowed be Thy name.
Thy kingdom come,
Thy will be done, on earth
As it is in Heaven.
Give us this day our daily bread,
And forgive us our debts,
As we forgive our debtors.
And lead us not into temptation,
But deliver us from evil.
For Thine is the kingdom,
And the power, and the glory,
Forever and ever.

Amen.

Praise God, from Whom all blessings flow;
Praise Him, all creatures here below;
Praise Him above, ye heavenly host;
Praise Father, Son, and Holy Ghost.

Amen.